Table of Conten

General Information

Baker Man
page 13

UFO Alien
page 26

Baby Bottle

Skill Level
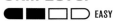 ◼◼◻▭ EASY

Finished Measurement
11 inches tall

Materials
- Red Heart Super Saver medium (worsted) weight acrylic yarn (7 oz/364 yds/198g per skein):
  - 1 skein each #311 white and #373 petal pink
- Caron One Pound medium (worsted) weight acrylic yarn (16 oz/812 yds/454g per skein):
  - 100 yds #10589 cream
- Aunt Lydia's Classic Crochet size 10 crochet cotton (400 yds per ball):
  - 1 ball #1 white
- Size H/8/5mm crochet hook or size needed to obtain gauge
- Size 7/1.65mm steel crochet hook
- Tapestry needle
- ¼-inch-wide pink ribbon: 2¼ yds
- Small amounts blue, black and red felt
- Craft glue
- Polyester fiberfill

Gauge
Size H hook: 4 sc = 1 inch; 3 sc rows = 1 inch

Pattern Notes
Weave in ends as work progresses.

Join with slip stitch as indicated unless otherwise stated.

After changing color, drop old color unless otherwise stated.

Chain-3 at beginning of round or row counts as first double crochet unless otherwise stated.

Special Stitch
Picot: Ch 4, sc in 4th ch from hook.

Baby
Rnd 1: Starting at top with size H hook and pink, ch 4, **join** *(see Pattern Notes)* in first ch to form ring, ch 1, 16 sc in ring, join in beg sc, turn. *(16 sc)*

Rnd 2: Ch 1, sc in each sc around, join in beg sc, turn.

Rnds 3–10: Rep rnd 2.

Rnd 11: Ch 1, [2 sc in next st, sc in each of next 7 sts] around, join in beg sc, turn. *(18 sc)*

Rnds 12 & 13: Rep rnd 2.

Rnd 14: Ch 1, [2 sc in next st, sc in each of next 2 sts] 3 times, **change color** *(see Stitch Guide and Pattern Notes)* to cream in last st, [2 sc in next st, sc in each of next 2 sts] 3 times, join in beg sc, turn. *(24 sc)*

Rnd 15: Ch 1, sc in each of next 12 sts, changing color to pink in last st, sc in each of last 12 sts, join in beg sc, turn.

Rnd 16: Ch 1, sc in each of next 12 sts, changing color to cream in last st, sc in each of last 12 sts, join in beg sc, turn.

Rnd 17: Ch 1, [sk next st, sc in each of next 3 sts] 3 times, changing color to pink in last st, [sk next st, sc in each of next 3 sts] 3 times, join in beg sc, turn. *(18 sc)*

Rnd 18: Ch 1, sc in each of next 9 sts, changing color to cream in last st, sc in each of last 9 sts, join in beg sc, turn.

Rnd 19: Ch 1, [sk next st, sc in each of next 2 sts] 3 times, changing color to pink in last st, [sk next st, sc in each of next 3 sc] 3 times, join in beg sc, turn. *(12 sc)*

Rnd 20: Ch 1, sc in each of next 6 sts, changing color to cream in last st, sc in each of last 6 sts, join in beg sc, turn.

Rnds 21 & 22: Rep rnd 2. At end of last rnd, change color to pink in last st, turn. Fasten off cream.

Rnd 23: Ch 1, 2 sc in each st around, join in beg sc, turn. *(24 sc)*

Stuff with fiberfill.

Rnd 24: Ch 1, [2 sc next st, sc in each of next 5 sts] around, join in beg sc, turn. *(28 sc)*

Rnds 25–27: Rep rnd 2.

Rnd 28: Ch 1, [2 sc in next st, sc in each of next 6 sts] around, join in beg sc, turn. *(32 sc)*

Rnds 29 & 30: Rep rnd 2.

Rnd 31: Ch 1, [2 sc in next st, sc in each of next 7 sts] around, join in beg sc, turn. *(36 sc)*

Rnds 32–35: Rep rnd 2.

Rnd 36: Ch 1, [2 sc next st, sc in each of next 5 sts] around, join in beg sc, turn. *(42 sc)*

Rnds 37–44: Rep rnd 2.

Rnd 45: Ch 3 *(see Pattern Notes)*, dc in same st as beg ch-3, dc in next st, [2 dc in next st, dc in next st] around, join in 3rd ch of beg ch-3, turn. *(63 dc)*

Rnd 46: Ch 3, dc in same st as beg ch-3, dc in each of next 2 sts, [2 dc in next st, dc in each of next 2 sts] around, join in 3rd ch of beg ch-3. Fasten off. *(84 dc)*

Finish stuffing.

Bottom

Rnd 1: With size H hook and pink, ch 4, join in first ch to form ring, ch 1, 12 sc in ring, join in beg sc, turn. *(12 sc)*

Rnds 2 & 3: Ch 1, [2 sc in next st, sc in next sc] around, join in beg sc, turn. *(27 sc at end of last rnd)*

Rnd 4: Ch 1, [2 sc in next st, sc in each of next 2 sc] around, join in beg sc, turn. *(36 sc)*

Rnd 5: Ch 1, [2 sc in next st, sc in each of next 3 sc] around, join in beg sc, turn. *(45 sc)*

Rnd 6: Ch 3, dc in each rem sc around, join in 3rd ch of beg ch-3, turn.

Rnd 7: Ch 3, dc in same st as beg ch-3, dc in each of next 3 dc, [2 sc in next st, sc in each of next 3 dc] around, join in 3rd ch of beg ch-3, turn. *(56 sc)*

Rnd 8: Ch 3, dc in same st as beg ch-3, dc in each of next 3 sts, [2 dc in next st, dc in each of next 3 sts] around, join in 3rd ch of beg ch-3. Fasten off. *(70 dc)*

Collar

Row 1: With size 7 steel hook and white thread, ch 4, sc in 2nd ch from hook, sc in each rem ch across, turn. *(3 sc)*

Row 2: Ch 1, 2 sc in first sc, sc in each of last 2 sc, turn. *(4 sc)*

Row 3: Ch 1, sc in each of first 3 sc, 2 sc in last sc, turn. *(5 sc)*

Row 4: Ch 1, 2 sc in first sc, sc in each rem sc across, turn. *(6 sc)*

Row 5: Ch 1, sc in each sc across, turn.

Row 6: Rep row 5.

Row 7: Ch 1, sc in each of first 4 sc, sk next sc, sc in last sc, turn. *(5 sc)*

Row 8: Ch 1, sk first sc, sc in each of next 4 sc, turn. *(4 sc)*

Row 9: Ch 1, sc in each of first 2 sc, sk next sc, sc in last sc, turn. *(3 sc)*

Rows 10–47: Rep row 5.

Row 48: Ch 1, sc in each of first 2 sc, 2 sc in last sc, turn. *(4 sc)*

Row 49: Ch 1, 2 sc in first sc, sc in each of next 3 sc, turn. *(5 sc)*

Row 50: Ch 1, sc in each of first 4 sc, 2 sc in last sc, turn. *(6 sc)*

Rows 51 & 52: Rep row 5.

Row 53: Ch 1, sk first sc, sc in each of next 5 sc, turn. *(5 sc)*

Row 54: Ch 1, sc in each of first 3 sc, sk next sc, sc in last sc, turn. *(4 sc)*

Row 55: Ch 1, sk first sc, sc in each of next 3 sc, turn. *(3 sc)*

Edging

Ch 1, working around outer edge, sc in each st and end of each row, working 3 sc in each corner, join in beg sc. Fasten off.

Button
Make 3.

Rnd 1: With size 7 steel hook and white thread, ch 3, join in first ch to form ring, ch 1, 8 sc in ring, join in beg sc, turn. *(8 sc)*

Rnd 2: Ch 1, [2 sc in next sc, sc in next sc] around, join in beg sc, turn. *(12 sc)*

Rnd 3: Ch 1, sc in each sc around, join in beg sc, turn.

Rnd 4: Ch 1, [sk next st, sc in next sc] around, join in beg sc. Fasten off. *(6 sc)*

Bonnet Trim

Row 1: With size 7 steel hook and white thread, ch 8, dc in 4th ch from hook *(beg 3 sk chs count as a dc)*, ch 2, sk next 2 chs, dc in each of last 2 chs, turn. *(4 dc, 1 ch-2 sp)*

Row 2: Ch 3, dc in next dc, ch 2, sk next ch-2 sp, dc in each of last 2 dc, turn.

Rows 3–28: Rep row 2. At end of last row, do not turn.

Row 29: Ch 1, working across bottom edge, work 3 sc in end of each row across, turn.

Row 30: [Ch 4, sl st in next st, ch 3, sl st in next st] across. Fasten off.

Bottom Trim

Row 1: With size 7 steel hook and white thread, ch 8, dc in 4th ch from hook *(beg 3 sk chs count as a dc)*, ch 2, sk next 2 chs, dc in each of last 2 chs, turn. *(4 dc, 1 ch-2 sp)*

Row 2: Picot *(see Special Stitch)*, dc in each of first 2 sts, ch 2, sk next ch-2 sp, dc in each of last 2 sts, turn.

Row 3: Ch 3, dc in next st, ch 2, sk next ch-2 sp, dc in each of last 2 sts, turn.

Row 4: Picot, dc in each of first 2 sts, ch 2, sk next ch-2 sp, dc in each of last 2 sts, ch 1, do not turn, working across next side in ends of rows, sk first row, (3 dc, ch 2, 3 dc) in next row, ch 1, sl st in next row, turn.

Row 5: Ch 1, sc in first ch-1 sp, sc in each of next 3 sts, (sc, picot, sc) in next ch-2 sp, sc in each of next 3 sts, sc in next ch-1 sp, sl st in next dc, ch 3, dc in next st, ch 2, sk next ch-2 sp, dc in each of last 2 sts, turn.

Row 6: Picot, dc in each of first 2 sts, ch 2, sk next ch-2 sp, dc in each of next 2 sts, leave rem sts unworked, turn.

Rows 7–50: [Rep rows 3–6] 11 times.

Row 51: Rep row 3.

Row 52: Picot, dc in each of first 2 sts, ch 2, sk next ch-2 sp, dc in each of last 2 sts. Fasten off.

Sleeve
Make 2.

Rnd 1: With size H hook and pink, ch 4, join in first ch to form ring, ch 1, 12 sc in ring, join in beg sc, turn. *(12 sc)*

Rnd 2: Ch 1, sc in each sc around, join in beg sc, turn.

Rnds 3–9: Rep rnd 2.

Rnd 10: Ch 1, [sk next st, sc in next st] around, join in beg sc. Fasten off.

Row 11: Fold rnd 10 flat, now working in rows and through both thicknesses, join cream in folded end, ch 1, sc in same st as beg ch-1, sc in each of next 3 sc, turn. *(4 sc)*

Row 12: Ch 1, sc in each sc across, turn.

Row 13: Ch 1, sk first st, sc in next st, sk next st, sc in last st. Fasten off. *(2 sc)*

Sleeve Trim
Make 2.

Row 1: With size 7 steel hook and white thread, ch 8, dc in 4th ch from hook *(beg 3 sk chs count as a dc)*, ch 2, sk next 2 chs, dc in each of last 2 chs, turn. *(4 dc, 1 ch-2 sp)*

Row 2: Ch 3, dc in next st, ch 2, sk next ch-2 sp, dc in each of last 2 sts, turn.

Rows 3–14: Rep row 2. At end of last row, do not turn.

Edging
Row 15: Ch 1, working across bottom edge of trim, work 3 sc in end of each row across, turn.

Row 16: [Ch 4, sl st in next st, ch 3, sl st in next st] across. Fasten off.

Finishing
With pink, sew Bottom to end of Baby. Cut 2 small ovals from black felt and 2 slightly larger ovals from blue felt. Cut mouth shape from red felt. Referring to photo for placement, glue to Baby's face.

Sew Collar around Baby's neck.

Fasten Buttons to front of Baby by embroidering a **French knot** *(see illustration)* in center of each one.

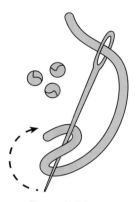

French Knot

Cut a 20-inch length of pink ribbon. Weave through Bonnet Trim. Sew trim across bottom edge of Bonnet where pink section meets cream section so that ribbon is at bottom. Tie ribbon in a bow and trim ends.

Cut a 25-inch length of pink ribbon. Beg at center back, weave through Bottom Trim. Sew trim around bottom edge of Baby. Tie ribbon in a bow and trim ends.

Sew 1 Sleeve to each side of Baby.

Cut 2 14-inch lengths of pink ribbon. Weave 1 length through Sleeve Trim. Sew around bottom edge of Sleeve above cream section. Tie ribbon in a bow and trim ends. Rep on other Sleeve.

Bottle

Bottom Ring

Rnd 1: With size H hook and white, ch 42, **join** *(see Pattern Notes)* in first ch to form ring, ch 1, sc in each ch around, join in beg sc, turn. *(42 sc)*

Rnd 2: Ch 1, sc in each sc around, join in beg sc, turn.

Rnds 3–78: Rep rnd 2. At end of last rnd, fasten off.

Stuff lightly and sew ends tog to form a ring.

Center Ring

Rnd 1: With size H hook and white, ch 22, join in first ch to form ring, ch 1, sc in each ch around, join in beg sc, turn. *(22 sc)*

Rnd 2: Ch 1, sc in each sc around, join in beg sc, turn.

Rnds 3–68: Rep rnd 2. At end of last rnd, fasten off.

Stuff lightly and sew ends tog to form a ring.

Top Ring

Rnd 1: With size H hook and pink, ch 26, join in first ch to form ring, ch 1, sc in each ch around, join in beg sc, turn. *(26 sc)*

Rnd 2: Ch 1, sc in each sc around, join in beg sc, turn.

Rnds 3–62: Rep rnd 2. At end of last rnd, fasten off.

Stuff lightly and sew ends tog to form a ring. ●

Cow Barn

Skill Level

 EASY

Finished Measurement

11 inches tall

Materials

- Red Heart Super Saver medium (worsted) weight acrylic yarn (7 oz/364 yds/198g per skein):
  1 skein #319 cherry red
  350 yds #313 Aran and #360 café latte
  100 yds #311 white and #312 black
- Size H/8/5mm crochet hook or size needed to obtain gauge
- Tapestry needle
- Small amounts black and white felt
- Craft glue
- Polyester fiberfill
- Stitch marker

Gauge

4 sc = 1 inch; 3 sc rows = 1 inch

Pattern Notes

Weave in ends as work progresses.

Join with slip stitch as indicated unless otherwise stated.

After changing color, drop old color unless otherwise stated.

Chain-3 at beginning of round counts as first double crochet unless otherwise stated.

Cow

Rnd 1: Starting at top with Aran, ch 4, **join** *(see Pattern Notes)* in first ch to form ring, ch 1, 12 sc in ring, join in beg sc, turn. *(12 sc)*

Rnd 2: Ch 1, [2 sc in next st, sc in next st] around, join in beg sc, ch-1, turn. *(18 sts)*

Rnd 3: Ch 1, sc in each st around, turn.

Rnds 4–8: Rep rnd 3.

Rnd 9: Ch 1, [2 sc in next st, sc in each of next 5 sts] around, join in beg sc, ch-1, turn. *(21 sts)*

Rnd 10: Ch 1, [2 sc in next st, sc in each of next 6 sts] around, join in beg sc, ch-1, turn. *(24 sts)*

Rnd 11: Rep rnd 3.

Rnd 12: Ch 1, [2 sc in next st, sc in each of next 3 sts] around, join in beg sc, ch-1, turn. *(30 sts)*

Rnds 13 & 14: Rep rnd 3.

Rnd 15: Ch 1, [sk next st, sc in each of next 4 sts] around, join in beg sc, turn. *(24 sts)*

Rnd 16: Ch 1, [sk next st, sc in each of next 3 sts] around, join in beg sc, turn. *(18 sts)*

Rnd 17: Ch 1, [sk next st, sc in each of next 2 sts] around, join in beg sc, turn. *(12 sts)*

Rnds 18 & 19: Rep rnd 3.

Rnd 20: Ch 1, 2 sc in each st around, join in beg sc, turn. *(24 sts)*

Stuff with fiberfill.

Rnd 21: Ch 1, [2 sc in next st, sc in each of next 5 sts] around, join in beg sc, ch-1, turn. *(28 sts)*

Rnds 22–26: Rep rnd 3.

Rnd 27: Ch 1, [2 sc in next st, sc in each of next 6 sts] around, join in beg sc, ch-1, turn. *(32 sts)*

Rnds 28 & 29: Rep rnd 3.

Rnd 30: Ch 1, [2 sc in next st, sc in each of next 7 sts] around, join in beg sc, ch-1, turn. *(36 sts)*

Rnds 31–34: Rep rnd 3.

Rnd 35: Ch 1, 2 sc in same st as beg ch-1, sc in each of next 5 sts, [2 sc in next st, sc in each of next 5 sts] around, join in beg sc, ch-1, turn. *(42 sts)*

Rnds 36–42: Rep rnd 3.

Rnd 43: Ch 1, sc in each st around, **change color** *(see Stitch Guide and Pattern Notes)* to café latte in last st, turn. Fasten off Aran.

Rnd 44: Ch 3 *(see Pattern Notes)*, dc in same st as beg ch-3, dc in next st, [2 dc in next st, dc in next st] around, join in 3rd ch of beg ch-3, turn. *(63 sts)*

Rnd 45: Ch 3, dc in same st as beg ch-3, dc in each of next 2 sts, [2 dc in next st, dc in each of next 2 sts] around, join in 3rd ch of beg ch-3. Fasten off. *(84 sts)*

Finish stuffing.

Bottom

Rnd 1: With café latte, ch 4, join to form ring, ch 1, 12 sc in ring, join in beg sc, turn. *(12 sts)*

Rnds 2 & 3: Ch 1, [2 sc in next st, sc in next st] around, join in beg sc, turn. *(27 sts at end of last rnd)*

Rnd 4: Ch 1, [2 sc in next st, sc in each of next 2 sts] around, join in beg sc, turn. *(36 sts)*

Rnd 5: Ch 1, [2 sc in next st, sc in each of next 3 sts] around, join in beg sc, turn. *(45 sts)*

Rnd 6: Ch 3, dc in each rem st around, join in 3rd ch of beg ch-3, turn.

Rnd 7: Ch 3, [2 dc in next st, dc in each of next 3 sts] around, join in 3rd ch of beg ch-3, turn. *(56 sts)*

Rnd 8: Ch 3, dc in same st as beg ch-3, dc in each of next 3 sts, [2 dc in next st, dc in each of next 3 sts] around, join in 3rd ch of beg ch-3. Fasten off. *(70 sts)*

Muzzle

Rnd 1: With café latte, ch 5, sc in 2nd ch from hook, sc in each of next 2 chs, 3 sc in last ch, working in unused lps on opposite side of foundation ch, sc in each of next 2 chs, 2 sc in last ch, join in beg sc, turn. *(10 sts)*

Rnd 2: Ch 1, 2 sc in each of next 2 sts, sc in each of next 2 sts, 2 sc in each of next 3 sts, sc in each of next 2 sts, 2 sc in last st, join in beg sc, turn. *(16 sts)*

Rnd 3: Ch 1, 2 sc in each of next 2 sts, sc in each of next 2 sts, 2 sc in each of next 6 sts, sc in each of next 2 sts, 2 sc in each of last 4 sts, join in beg sc. Fasten off. *(28 sts)*

Arm
Make 2.

Row 1: With café latte, ch 2, sc in 2nd ch from hook, turn. *(1 st)*

Row 2: Ch 1, 3 sc in same st as beg ch-1, turn. *(3 sts)*

Row 3: Ch 1, sc in each st across, changing color to Aran in last st, turn. Fasten off café latte.

Rows 4–8: Ch 1, sc in each st across, turn.

Row 9: Ch 1, sk first st, sc in each rem st across. Fasten off. *(2 sts)*

Edging
Hold Arm with foundation ch at top, join café latte in end of row 3 on right edge, ch 1, sc evenly sp around outer edge of café latte section, changing color to Aran in last st, sc evenly sp around Aran section, join in beg sc. Fasten off both colors.

Ear
Make 2.

Row 1: With Aran, ch 3, sc in 2nd ch from hook, sc in last ch, turn. *(2 sts)*

Rows 2 & 3: Ch 1, sc in each st across, turn.

Row 4: Ch 1, 2 sc in each st across, turn. *(4 sts)*

Row 5: Ch 1, 2 sc in first st, sc in each of next 2 sts, 2 sc in last st, turn. *(6 sts)*

Row 6: Ch 1, sc in each st across, turn.

Row 7: Ch 1, sk first st, sc in each of next 3 sts, sk next st, sc in last st, turn. *(4 sts)*

Row 8: Ch 1, sk first st, sc in next st, sk next st, sc in last st. Fasten off. *(2 sts)*

Fold Ears in half lengthwise and sew to top of Cow's head.

Hair
Rnd 1: With café latte, ch 3, join to form a ring, ch 1, 8 sc in ring, join in beg sc, turn. *(8 sts)*

Rnd 2: [Ch 8, sl st in next st] around, turn.

Rnd 3: Holding ch-8 sps to back of work, ch 1, [2 sc next st, sc next st] around, join in beg sc, turn. (12 sts)

Rnd 4: Rep rnd 2. Fasten off.

Tummy

Rnd 1: With café latte, ch 5, sc in 2nd ch from hook, sc in each of next 2 chs, 3 sc in next ch, working in unused lps on opposite side of foundation ch, sc in each of next 2 chs, 2 sc in last ch, join in beg sc, turn. *(10 sts)*

Rnd 2: Ch 1, 2 sc in each of next 2 sts, sc in each of next 2 sts, 2 sc in each of next 3 sts, 2 sc in each of next 2 sts, 2 sc in last st, join in beg sc, turn. *(16 sts)*

Rnd 3: Ch 1, 2 sc in each of next 2 sts, sc in each of next 2 sts, 2 sc in each of next 6 sts, sc in each of next 2 sts, 2 sc in each of last 4 sts, join in beg sc, turn. *(28 sts)*

Rnd 4: Ch 1, 2 sc in next st, sc in next st, [2 sc in next st, sc in next st] 4 times, sc in each of next 2 sts, [2 sc in next st, sc in next st] 6 times, sc in each of next 2 sts, [2 sc in next st, sc in next st] twice, join in beg sc. Fasten off. *(40 sts)*

Finishing

With café latte, sew Bottom to base of Cow.

With black and using **straight stitch** *(see illustration)* and **backstitch** *(see illustration)*, embroider nose and mouth on Muzzle. Sew Muzzle to Cow's face. Referring to photo for shapes, cut eyes from black and white felt and glue to Cow above Muzzle.

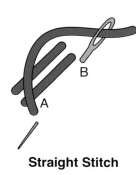

Straight Stitch

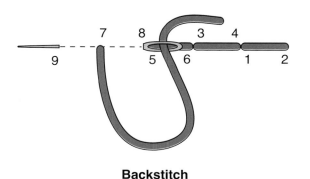

Backstitch

Sew one Arm to each side of Cow and Hair to top of Cow's head. Sew Tummy to front of Cow.

Barn

Bottom Ring

Rnd 1: With red, ch 42, **join** *(see Pattern Notes)* to form a ring, ch 1, sc in each ch around, join in beg sc, turn. *(42 sts)*

Rnds 2–78: Ch 1, sc in each st around, join in beg sc, turn. At end of last rnd, fasten off.

Stuff lightly and sew ends tog to form a ring.

Bottom of Barn Door

Row 1: With red, ch 21, sc in 2nd ch from hook, sc in each rem ch across, turn. *(20 sts)*

Rows 2–12: Ch 1, sc in each st across, turn. At end of last row, fasten off.

Side Trim

Join white in side of row 12, ch 1, working across side in ends of rows, sc evenly sp across side. Fasten off.

Rep on other side.

Inside Trim
Make 2.

Row 1: With white, ch 2, sc in 2nd ch from hook, turn. *(1 st)*

Rows 2–17: Ch 1, sc in st, turn. At end of last row, fasten off.

Center Ring
Rnd 1: With red, ch 22, join to form a ring, ch 1, sc in each ch around, join in beg sc, turn. *(22 sts)*

Rnds 2–68: Ch 1, sc in each st around, join in beg sc, turn. At end of last rnd, fasten off.

Stuff lightly and sew ends tog to form a ring.

Small Window
Make 4.

Row 1: With café latte, ch 6, sc in 2nd ch from hook, sc in each rem ch across, turn. *(5 sts)*

Rows 2–5: Ch 1, sc in each st across, turn. At end of last row, change color to white in last st. Fasten off café latte.

Trim
Ch 1, working around outer edge, sc in each st and in end of each row, working (sc, ch 2, sc) in each corner, join in beg sc. Fasten off.

Top of Barn Door
Row 1: With red, ch 21, sc in 2nd ch from hook, sc in each rem ch across, turn. *(20 sts)*

Rows 2–6: Ch 1, sc in each st across, turn. At end of last row, do not turn. Change color to white in last st. Fasten off red.

Trim
Working across next side in ends of rows, sc in each row across, (sc, ch 2, sc) in next corner, sc in each st across next side, (sc, ch 2, sc) in next corner, working across next side in ends of rows, sc in each row. Fasten off.

Inside Trim
Make 2.

Row 1: With white, ch 2, sc in 2nd ch from hook, turn. *(1 st)*

Rows 2–13: Ch 1, sc in each st across, turn. At end of last row, fasten off.

Top Ring
Rnd 1: With red, ch 26, join to form a ring, turn, ch 1, sc in each ch around, join in beg sc, turn. *(26 sts)*

Rnd 2–62: Ch 1, sc in each st around, join in beg sc, turn. At end of last rnd, fasten off.

Stuff lightly and sew ends tog to form a ring.

Window
Row 1: With café latte, ch 11, sc in 2nd ch from hook, sc in each rem ch across, turn. *(10 sts)*

Rows 2–6: Ch 1, sc in each st across, turn. At end of last row, change color to white in last st. Fasten off café latte.

Trim
Working around outer edge, sc in each st and in end of each row, working (sc, ch 2, sc) in each corner, join in beg sc. Fasten off.

Window Shutter
Make 2.

Row 1: With white, ch 5, sc in 2nd ch from hook, sc in each rem ch across, turn. *(4 sts)*

Rows 2–9: Ch 1, working in **back lps** *(see Stitch Guide)*, sc in each st across, turn. At end of last row, fasten off.

Finishing
Referring to photo for placement, sew Inside Trims to Bottom of Barn Door from bottom corners of Side Trim to center top edge. Sew Bottom of Barn Door to Bottom Ring.

Referring to photo for placement, sew Inside Trims to Top of Barn Door from top corners of Side Trim to center bottom edge. Sew Top of Barn Door to Center Ring.

Sew 2 Small Windows to each side of Top of Barn Door on Center Ring.

Sew Window to Top Ring and sew a Shutter to each side of Window. ●

Baker Man

Skill Level

◖◖◻◻◗ **EASY**

Finished Measurement

11 inches tall

Materials

- Red Heart Super Saver medium (worsted) weight acrylic yarn (7 oz/364 yds/198g per skein): 1 skein each #311 white, #319 cherry red, #312 black and #360 café latte
- Caron One Pound medium (worsted) weight acrylic yarn (16 oz/812 yds/454g per skein): 100 yds #10589 cream
- Size H/8/5mm crochet hook or size needed to obtain gauge
- Tapestry needle
- Small amounts black and other various colors of felt
- Craft glue
- Polyester fiberfill

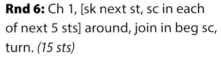

Need help?
StitchGuide.com
ILLUSTRATED GUIDES
HOW-TO VIDEOS

Gauge

4 sc = 1 inch; 3 sc rows = 1 inch

Pattern Notes

Weave in ends as work progresses.

Join with slip stitch as indicated unless otherwise stated.

After changing color, drop old color. Do not fasten off unless otherwise stated.

Chain-3 at beginning of round counts as first double crochet unless otherwise stated.

Baker Man

Rnd 1: Starting at top of hat with red, ch 4, **join** *(see Pattern Notes)* in first ch to form ring, ch 1, 12 sc in ring, join in beg sc, turn. *(12 sts)*

Rnd 2: Ch 1, 2 sc in each st around, join in beg sc, turn. *(24 sts)*

Rnd 3: Ch 1, [2 sc in next st, sc in next st] around, join in beg sc, turn. *(36 sts)*

Rnd 4: Ch 1, sc in each st around, join in beg sc, turn.

Rnd 5: Ch 1, [sk next st, sc in next st] around, join in beg sc, turn. *(18 sts)*

Rnd 6: Ch 1, [sk next st, sc in each of next 5 sts] around, join in beg sc, turn. *(15 sts)*

Rnds 7–9: Rep rnd 4. At end of rnd 9, **change color** *(see Stitch Guide and Pattern Notes)* to black in last st, turn. Fasten off red.

Rnd 10: Ch 1, [2 sc in next st, sc in each of next 4 sts] around, join in beg sc, turn. *(18 sts)*

Rnd 11: Ch 1, [2 sc in next st, sc in each of next 2 sts] twice, changing color to cream in last st, [2 sc in next st, sc in each of next 2 sts] 3 times, join in beg sc, turn. *(24 sts)*

Rnd 12: Ch 1, sc in each of next 12 sts, changing color to black in last sc, sc in each of last 12 sts, join in beg sc, turn.

Rnd 13: Ch 1, sc in each of next 12 sts, changing color to cream in last sc, sc in each of last 12 sts, join in beg sc, turn.

Rnd 14: Ch 1, [sk next st, sc in each of next 3 sts] 3 times, changing color to black in last st, [sk next st, sc in each of next 3 sts] 3 times, join in beg sc, turn. *(18 sts)*

Rnd 15: Ch 1, sc in each of next 9 sts, changing color to cream in last st, sc in each of last 9 sts, join in beg sc, turn.

Rnd 16: Ch 1, [sk next st, sc in each of next 2 sts] 3 times, changing color to black in last st, [sk next st, sc in each of next 2 sts] 3 times, join in beg sc, turn. *(12 sts)*

Rnd 17: Ch 1, sc in each of next 6 sts, changing color to cream in last st, sc in each of last 6 sts, join in beg sc, turn. Fasten off black.

Rnd 18: Rep rnd 4.

Rnd 19: Ch 1, sc in each st around, join in beg sc, changing color to white in last st, turn. Fasten off cream.

Rnd 20: Ch 1, 2 sc in each st around, join in beg sc, turn. *(24 sts)*

Stuff with fiberfill.

Rnd 21: Ch 1, [2 sc in next st, sc in each of next 5 sts] around, join in beg sc, turn. *(28 sts)*

Rnds 22–26: Rep rnd 4.

Rnd 27: Ch 1, [2 sc in next st, sc in each of next 6 sts] around, join in beg sc, turn. *(32 sts)*

Rnds 28 & 29: Rep rnd 4.

Rnd 30: Ch 1, [2 sc in next st, sc in each of next 7 sts] around, join in beg sc, turn. *(36 sts)*

Rnds 31–34: Rep rnd 4.

Rnd 35: Ch 1, [2 sc in next st, sc in each of next 5 sts] around, join in beg sc, turn. *(42 sts)*

Rnds 36–42: Rep rnd 4.

Rnd 43: Ch 1, sc in each st around, join in beg sc, changing color to black in last st, turn. Fasten off white.

Rnd 44: Ch 3 *(see Pattern Notes)*, dc in same st as beg ch-3, dc in next st, [2 dc in next st, dc in next st] around, join in 3rd ch of beg ch-3, turn. *(63 sts)*

Rnd 45: Ch 3, dc in same st as beg ch-3, dc in each of next 2 sts, [2 dc in next st, dc in each of next 2 sts] around, join in 3rd ch of beg ch-3. Fasten off. *(84 sts)*

Finish stuffing.

Bottom

Rnd 1: With black, ch 4, join to form a ring, ch 1, 12 sc in ring, join in beg sc, turn. *(12 sts)*

Rnds 2 & 3: Ch 1, [2 sc in next st, sc in next st] around, join in beg sc, turn. *(27 sts at end of last rnd)*

Rnd 4: Ch 1, [2 sc in next st, sc in each of next 2 sts] around, join in beg sc, turn. *(36 sts)*

Rnd 5: Ch 1, [2 sc in next st, sc in each of next 3 sts] around, join in beg sc, turn. *(45 sts)*

Rnd 6: Ch 3, dc in each st around, join in beg ch-3, turn.

Rnd 7: Ch 3, [2 dc next st, dc in each of next 3 sts] around, join in 3rd ch of beg ch-3, turn. *(56 sts)*

Rnd 8: Ch 3, dc in same st as beg ch-3, dc in each of next 3 sts, [2 dc next st, dc in each of next 3 sts] around, join in beg ch-3. Fasten off. *(70 sts)*

Hat Band
Row 1: With red, ch 3, sc in 2nd ch from hook, sc in last ch, turn. *(2 sts)*

Rows 2–24: Ch 1, sc in each st across, turn. At end of last row, fasten off.

Scarf
With red, ch 36. Fasten off.

Apron
Row 1: With red, ch 17, sc in 2nd ch from hook, sc in each rem ch across, turn. *(16 sts)*

Rows 2–6: Ch 1, sc in each st across, turn.

Rows 7–10: Ch 1, sk first st, sc in each st across to last 2 sts, sk next st, sc in last st, turn. *(8 sts at end of last row)*

Edging
Ch 1, working around outer edge, sc evenly sp around, working 3 sc in each corner, join in beg sc. Fasten off.

Arm
Make 2.

Row 1: With cream, ch 2, sc in 2nd ch from hook, turn. *(1 st)*

Row 2: Ch 1, 3 sc in same st as beg ch-1, turn. *(3 sts)*

Row 3: Ch 1, sc in each st across, changing color to white in last st, turn. Fasten off cream.

Rows 4–8: Ch 1, sc in each st across, turn.

Row 9: Ch 1, sk first st, sc in each rem st across. Fasten off. *(2 sts)*

Edging
Hold Arm with foundation ch at top, join cream in end of row 3, ch 1, sc evenly sp around outer edge of cream section, change color to white in last sc, sc evenly sp around white section, join in beg sc. Fasten off both colors.

Finishing
With black, sew Bottom to base of Baker Man. Using black felt, cut 2 small circles for eyes and 2 curved pieces for mustache. Referring to photo for placement, glue pieces to face.

Sew one Arm to each side of Baker Man and Apron to front of Baker Man at waist. Sew Hat Band around hat where red section meets black section.

Tie Scarf around neck.

Continued on page 30

Race Car Driver

Finished Measurement

11 inches tall

Materials

- Red Heart Super Saver medium (worsted) weight acrylic yarn (7 oz/364 yds/198g per skein):
  - 2 skeins #885 delft blue
  - 150 yds each #319 cherry red, #312 black and #400 grey heather
- Caron One Pound medium (worsted) weight acrylic yarn (16 oz/812 yds/454g per skein):
  - 100 yds #10589 cream
- Size H/8/5mm crochet hook or size needed to obtain gauge
- Tapestry needle
- Small amounts black, red and white felt
- Craft glue
- Polyester fiberfill
- Straight pins

Gauge

4 sc = 1 inch; 3 sc rows = 1 inch

Pattern Notes

Weave in ends as work progresses.

Join with slip stitch as indicated unless otherwise stated.

After changing color, drop old color unless otherwise stated.

Chain-3 at beginning of round counts as a double crochet unless otherwise stated.

Driver

Rnd 1: Starting at top with blue, ch 4, **join** (see Pattern Notes) in first ch to form ring, ch 1, 12 sc in ring, join in beg sc, turn. (12 sc)

Rnd 2: Ch 1, [2 sc in next st, sc in next st] around, join in beg sc, turn. (18 sts)

Rnd 3: Ch 1, [2 sc in next st, sc in each of next 2 sts] around, join in beg sc, turn. (24 sts)

Rnd 4: Ch 1, sc in each st around, join in beg sc, turn.

Rnds 5–8: Rep rnd 4.

Rnd 9: Ch 1, sc in in each of next 16 sts, **change color** (see Stitch Guide and Pattern Notes) to cream in last st, sc in each of last 8 sts, join in beg sc, turn.

Rnd 10: Ch 1, sc in each of next 8 sts, changing color to blue in last st, sc in each of last 16 sts, join in beg sc, turn.

Rnd 11: Ch 1, sc in each of next 16 sts, changing color to cream in last sc, sc in each of last 8 sts, join in beg sc, turn.

Rnds 12 & 13: Rep rnds 10 and 11.

Rnd 14: Ch 1, sc in each of next 3 sts, changing color to blue in last st, carry cream behind work, sc in each of next 2 sts, changing color to cream in last st, carry blue, sc in each of next 3 sts, changing color to blue in last st, drop cream, sc in each of last 16 sts, turn.

Rnd 15: Ch 1, sc in each of next 16 sts, changing color to cream in last st, carry blue, sc in each of next 2 sts, changing color to blue, carry cream, sc in each of next 4 sts, changing color to cream, carry blue, sc in each of next 2 sts, changing color to blue in last st, join in beg sc, turn. Fasten off cream.

Rnd 16: Rep rnd 4.

Rnd 17: Ch 1, [sk next st, sc in each of next 2 sts] around, join in beg sc, turn. (16 sts)

Rnd 18: Ch 1, [sk next st, sc in each of next 3 sts] around, join cream in last st, join in beg sc, turn. Fasten off blue. (12 sts)

Rnd 19: Ch 1, sc in each st around, changing color to red in last st, join in beg sc, turn. Fasten off cream.

Rnd 20: Ch 1, 2 sc in each st around, join in beg sc, turn. (24 sts)

Stuff with fiberfill.

Rnd 21: Ch 1, [2 sc in next st, sc in each of next 5 sts] around, join in beg sc, turn. (28 sts)

Rnds 22–26: Rep rnd 4.

Rnd 27: Ch 1, [2 sc in next st, sc in each of next 6 sts] around, join in beg sc, turn. (32 sts)

Rnds 28 & 29: Rep rnd 4.

Rnd 30: Ch 1, [2 sc in next st, sc in each of next 7 sts] around, join in beg sc, turn. (36 sts)

Rnds 31–34: Rep rnd 4.

Rnd 35: Ch 1, [2 sc in next st, sc in each of next 5 sts] around, join in beg sc, turn. (42 sts)

Rnds 36–43: Rep rnd 4. At end of rnd 43, change color to blue in last st, turn. Fasten off red.

Rnd 44: Ch 3 (see Pattern Notes), dc in same st as beg ch-3, dc in next st, [2 dc next st, dc in next st] around, join in 3rd ch of beg ch-3, turn. (63 sts)

Rnd 45: Ch 3, dc in same st as beg ch-3, dc in each of next 2 sts, [2 dc in next st, dc in each of next 2 sts] around, join in 3rd ch of beg ch-3. Fasten off. *(84 sts)*

Finish stuffing.

Bottom
Rnd 1: With blue, ch 4, join to form ring, ch 1, 12 sc in ring, join in beg sc, turn. *(12 sts)*

Rnds 2 & 3: Ch 1, [2 sc in next st, sc in next st] around, join in beg sc, turn. *(27 sts at end of last rnd)*

Rnd 4: Ch 1, [2 sc in next st, sc in each of next 2 sts] around, join in beg sc, turn. *(36 sts)*

Rnd 5: Ch 1, [2 sc in next st, sc in each of next 3 sts] around, join in beg sc, turn. *(45 sts)*

Rnd 6: Ch 3, dc in each rem st around, join in 3rd ch of beg ch-3, turn.

Rnd 7: Ch 3, dc in same st as beg ch-3, dc in each of next 3 sts, [2 dc in next st, dc in each of next 3 sts] around, join in 3rd ch of beg ch-3, turn. *(56 sts)*

Rnd 8: Ch 3, dc same st as beg ch-3, [dc in each of next 3 sts, 2 dc in next st] around, ending with dc in each of last 3 sts, join in 3rd ch of beg ch-3. Fasten off. *(70 sts)*

Arm
Make 2.

Row 1: With cream, ch 2, sc in 2nd ch from hook, turn. *(1 st)*

Row 2: Ch 1, 3 sc in same st as beg ch-1, turn. *(3 sts)*

Row 3: Ch 1, sc in each st across, change color to red in last st, turn. Fasten off cream.

Rows 4–8: Ch 1, sc in each st across, turn.

Row 9: Ch 1, sk first st, sc in each of next 2 sts. Fasten off. *(2 sts)*

Edging
Hold Arm with foundation ch at top, join cream in side of row 3 at right edge, ch 1, sc evenly sp around cream section, changing color to red in last st, sc evenly sp around red section, join in beg sc. Fasten off both colors.

Driver's Belt
Row 1: With blue, ch 2, sc in 2nd ch from hook, turn. *(1 st)*

Rows 2–42: Ch 1, sc in same st as beg ch-1, turn. At end of row 42, fasten off.

Driver's Side Leg Stripe
Make 2.

Row 1: With blue, ch 2, sc in 2nd ch from hook, turn. *(1 st)*

Rows 2–13: Ch 1, sc in same st as beg ch-1, turn. At end of row 13, fasten off.

Collar
Row 1: With blue, ch 2, sc in 2nd ch from hook, turn. *(1 st)*

Rows 2–5: Ch 1, sc in same st as beg ch-1, turn.

Row 6: Ch 1, 3 sc in same st as beg ch-1, turn. *(3 sts)*

Row 7: Ch 1, 2 sc in first st, sc in each of next 2 sts, turn. *(4 sts)*

Row 8: Ch 1, sc in first st, leaving rem sts unworked, turn. *(1 st)*

Row 9: Ch 1, sc in same st as beg ch-1, turn.

Rows 10–18: Rep row 9.

Row 19: Rep row 6.

Row 20: Ch 1, 2 sc in first st, sc in each of last 2 sts, turn. *(4 sts)*

Row 21: Ch 1, sl st in first 3 sts, sc in last st, turn. *(1 st)*

Rows 22–25: Rep row 9. At end of last row, fasten off.

Number One
With blue, ch 5, sl st in 2nd ch from hook, sl st in each rem ch across. Fasten off.

Number Zero
With blue, ch 10, join to form ring, ch 1, turn, sl st in each ch around. Fasten off.

Finishing
Sew Bottom to bottom of Driver. With blue and using **backstitch** *(see illustration)*, embroider around face opening of Driver's helmet. Referring to photo for shapes, cut eyes from white felt and mouth from red felt. Glue pieces to Driver's face.

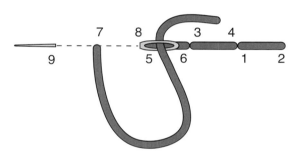

Backstitch

Sew Arm to each side of Driver.

Sew a Stripe to each side of Driver pants. Sew Belt around Driver's waist, making sure to cover top of each Stripe.

Sew Collar around Driver's neck, sewing ends into a V-shape at center front.

Sew One and Zero to front of Driver to form number "10."

Car

Bottom Ring
Rnd 1: With blue, ch 42, join to form a ring, ch 1, sc in each ch around, join in beg sc, turn. *(42 sts)*

Rnds 2–78: Ch 1, sc in each st around, join in beg sc, turn. At end of last rnd, fasten off.

Stuff lightly and sew ends tog to form a ring.

Wheel
Make 4.

Rnd 1: With gray, ch 3, join to form ring, ch 1, 12 sc in ring, join in beg sc, turn. *(12 sts)*

Rnd 2: Ch 1, [2 sc in next st, sc in next st] around, change color to black in last st, join in beg sc, turn. Fasten off gray. *(18 sts)*

Rnd 3: Ch 1, [2 sc in next st, sc in next st] around, join in beg sc, turn. *(27 sts)*

Rnd 4: Ch 1, sc in each st around, join in beg sc, turn.

Rnd 5: Ch 1, [2 sc in next st, sc in each of next 2 sts] around, change color to black in last st, join in beg sc, turn. *(36 sts)*

Rnd 6: Ch 1, sc in each st around, join in beg sc. Fasten off.

Bumper
Make 2.

Rnd 1: With gray, ch 19, sc in 2nd ch from hook, sc in each of next 16 chs, 3 sc in last ch, working in unused lps on opposite side of foundation ch, sc in each of next 16 chs, 2 sc in last ch, join in beg sc, turn. *(38 sts)*

Rnd 2: Ch 1, 2 sc in each of next 2 sts, sc in each of next 16 sts, 2 sc in each of next 3 sts, sc in each of next 16 sts, 2 sc in last st, join in beg sc. Fasten off. *(44 sts)*

Headlight
Make 4 white.

Row 1: With white, ch 6, sc in 2nd ch from hook, sc in each rem ch across, turn. *(5 sts)*

Row 2: Ch 1, sc in first st, hdc in next st, 3 dc in next st, hdc in next st, sc in last st. Fasten off. *(7 sts)*

Taillight
Make 4 red.

Row 1: With red, ch 6, sc in 2nd ch from hook, sc in each rem ch across, turn. *(5 sts)*

Row 2: Ch 1, sc in first st, hdc in next st, 3 dc in next st, hdc in next st, sc in last st. Fasten off. *(7 sts)*

Center Ring
Rnd 1: With blue, ch 22, join to form a ring, ch 1, sc in each ch around, join in beg sc, turn. *(22 sts)*

Rnds 2–68: Ch 1, sc in each st around, join in beg sc, turn. At end of last rnd, fasten off.

Stuff lightly and sew ends tog to form a ring.

Windshield Bottom
Make 2.

Row 1: With gray, ch 20, sc in 2nd ch from hook, sc in each rem ch across, turn. *(19 sts)*

Rows 2 & 3: Ch 1, sc in each sc across, turn. At end of last row, fasten off.

Top Ring
Rnd 1: With blue, ch 26, join to form ring, turn, sc in each ch around, join in beg sc, turn. *(26 sts)*

Rnds 2–62: Ch 1, sc in each st around, join in beg sc, turn. At end of last rnd, fasten off.

Stuff lightly and sew ends tog to form a ring.

Windshield Top
Make 2.

Row 1: With gray, ch 10, sc in 2nd ch from hook, sc in each rem ch across, turn. *(9 sts)*

Row 2: Ch 1, 2 sc in first st, sc in each rem st across to last st, 2 sc in last st, turn. *(11 sts)*

Rows 3–6: Rep row 2. *(19 sts at end of last row)*

Row 7: Ch 1, sc in each st across. Fasten off.

Side Window
Make 2.

Row 1: With gray, ch 7, sc in 2nd ch from hook, sc in each rem ch across, turn. *(6 sts)*

Rows 2–6: Ch 1, sc in each st across, turn. At end of last row, fasten off.

Number One
Make 2.

With red, ch 5, sl st in 2nd ch from hook, sl st in each rem ch across. Fasten off.

Number Zero
Make 2.

With red, ch 10, join to form ring, ch 1, turn, sl st in each ch around. Fasten off.

Finishing
Referring to photo for placement, sew Wheels to Bottom Ring and sew 1 Bumper between each pair of Wheels, curving slightly.

Sew 2 Headlights to Bottom Ring above Bumper and at top edge of ring for front of car. Sew 2 Taillights above 2nd Bumper at top edge of ring for back of car.

Place Center Ring over Bottom Ring. Pin rem Headlights and Taillights to Center Ring matching ones on Bottom Ring. Sew in place.

Sew 1 Windshield Bottom between Headlights and 1 between Taillights at top edge of Center Ring.

Sew One and Zero on each side of Center Ring to form car's number "10."

Place Top Ring over Center Ring and pin Windshield Top to Top Ring, matching Windshield Bottom on Center Ring. Sew in place.

Sew Windows to Top Ring over car numbers on Center Ring. ●

Frog Princess

Skill Level

■■■□□ EASY

Finished Measurement

11 inches tall

Materials

- Red Heart Super Saver medium (worsted) weight acrylic yarn (7 oz/364 yds/198g per skein): 1 skein each #406 medium thyme, #661 frosty green, #319 cherry red, #312 black and #579 pale plum
- Caron One Pound medium (worsted) weight acrylic yarn (16 oz/812 yds/454g per skein): 100 yds #10589 cream
- Size H/8/5mm crochet hook or size needed to obtain gauge
- Tapestry needle
- Small amounts blue, black and red felt
- Craft glue
- Polyester fiberfill

Gauge

4 sc = 1 inch; 3 sc rows = 1 inch

Pattern Notes

Weave in ends as work progresses.

Join with slip stitch as indicated unless otherwise stated.

After changing color, drop old color unless otherwise stated.

Chain-3 at beginning of round counts as a double crochet unless otherwise stated.

Princess

Rnd 1: Starting at top with red, ch 4, **join** (see Pattern Notes) in first ch to form ring, ch 1, 12 sc in ring, join in beg sc, turn. *(12 sc)*

Rnd 2: Ch 1, 2 sc in each st around, join in beg sc, turn. *(24 sts)*

Rnd 3: Ch 1, [2 sc in next st, sc in next st] around, join in beg sc, turn. *(36 sts)*

Rnd 4: Ch 1, sc in each st around, join in beg sc, turn.

Rnd 5: Ch 1, [sk next st, sc in next st] around, join in beg sc, turn. *(18 sts)*

Rnd 6: Ch 1, [sk next st, sc in each of next 5 sts] around, join in beg sc, turn. *(15 sts)*

Rnds 7–9: Rep rnd 4. At end of last rnd, **change color** *(see Stitch Guide and Pattern Notes)* to black in last st, turn. Fasten off red.

Rnd 10: Ch 1, [2 sc in next st, sc in each of next 4 sts] around, join in beg sc, turn. *(18 sts)*

Rnd 11: Ch 1, [2 sc in next st, sc in each of next 2 sts] 3 times, changing color to cream in last st, [2 sc in next st, sc in each of next 2 sts] 3 times, join in beg sc, turn. *(24 sts)*

Rnd 12: Ch 1, sc in each of next 12 sts, changing color to black in last st, sc in each of last 12 sts, join in beg sc, turn.

Rnd 13: Ch 1, sc in each of next 12 sts, changing color to cream in last st, sc in each of last 12 sts, join in beg sc, turn.

Rnd 14: Ch 1, [sk next st, sc in each of next 3 sts] 3 times, changing color to black in last st, [sk next st, sc in each of next 3 sts] 3 times, join in beg sc, turn. *(18 sts)*

Rnd 15: Ch 1, sc in each of next 9 sts, changing color to cream in last st, sc in each of last 9 sts, join in beg sc, turn.

Rnd 16: Ch 1, [sk next st, sc in each of next 2 sts] 3 times, changing color to black in last st, [sk next st, sc in each of next 2 sts] 3 times, join in beg sc, turn. *(12 sts)*

Rnd 17: Ch 1, sc in each of next 6 sts, changing color to cream in last st, sc in each of last 6 sts, join in beg sc, turn.

Rnds 18 & 19: Rep rnd 4. At end of last rnd, change color to plum in last st, turn. Fasten off black and cream.

Rnd 20: Ch 1, 2 sc in each around, join in beg sc, turn. *(24 sts)*

Stuff with fiberfill.

Rnd 21: Ch 1, [2 sc in next st, sc in each of next 5 sts] around, join in beg sc, turn. *(28 sts)*

Rnds 22–26: Rep rnd 4.

Rnd 27: Ch 1, [2 sc in next st, sc in each of next 6 sts] around, join in beg sc, turn. *(32 sts)*

Rnds 28 & 29: Rep rnd 4.

Rnd 30: Ch 1, [2 sc in next st, sc in each of next 7 sts] around, join in beg sc, turn. *(36 sts)*

Rnds 31–34: Rep rnd 4.

Rnd 35: Ch 1, [2 sc in next st, sc in each of next 5 sts] around, join in beg sc, turn. *(42 sts)*

Rnds 36–43: Rep rnd 4.

Rnd 44: Ch 3 *(see Pattern Notes)*, dc in same st as beg ch-3, dc in next st, [2 dc in next st, dc in next st] around, join in 3rd ch of beg ch-3, turn. *(63 sts)*

Rnd 45: Ch 3, dc in same st as beg ch-3, dc in each of next 2 sts, [2 dc in next st, dc in each of next 2 sts] around, join in 3rd ch of beg ch-3. Fasten off. *(84 sts)*

Finish stuffing.

Bottom

Rnd 1: With plum, ch 4, join in first ch to form ring, ch 1, 12 sc in ring, join in beg sc, turn. *(12 sts)*

Rnds 2 & 3: Ch 1, [2 sc in next st, sc in next st] around, join in beg sc, turn. *(27 sts at end of last rnd)*

Rnd 4: Ch 1, [2 sc in next st, sc in each of next 2 sts] around, join in beg sc, turn. *(36 sts)*

Rnd 5: Ch 1, [2 sc in next st, sc in each of next 3 sts] around, join in beg sc, turn. *(45 sts)*

Rnd 6: Ch 3, dc in each st around, join in 3rd ch of beg ch-3, turn.

Rnd 7: Ch 3, [2 dc in next st, dc in each of next 3 sts] around, join in 3rd ch of beg ch-3, turn. *(56 sts)*

Rnd 8: Ch 3, dc in same st as beg ch-3, dc in each of next 3 sts, [2 dc in next st, dc in each of next 3 sts] around, join in 3rd ch of beg ch-3. Fasten off. *(70 sts)*

Hair Bun

Rnd 1: With black, ch 6, sc in 2nd ch from hook, sc in each of next 3 chs, 3 sc in last ch, working in unused lps on opposite side of foundation ch, sc in each of next 3 chs, 2 sc in last ch, join in beg sc, turn. *(12 sts)*

Rnd 2: Ch 1, 2 sc in each of next 2 sts, sc in each of next 3 sts, 2 sc in each of next 3 sts, sc in each of next 3 sts, 2 sc in last st, join in beg sc, turn. *(18 sts)*

Rnds 3–5: Ch 1, sc in each st around, join in beg sc, turn. At end of last rnd, fasten off.

Crown

Row 1: With white, ch 20, sc in 2nd ch from hook, sc in each rem ch across, turn. *(19 sts)*

Row 2: Ch 1, sc in each st across, turn.

Row 3: *Ch 10, sl st in 4th ch from hook, [ch 4, sl st in 4th ch from hook] twice, ch 6 sk next 2 sts, sl st in next st, rep from * 5 times. Fasten off.

Collar

With white, ch 26, sl st in 4th ch from hook, [ch 3, sl st in next ch, ch 4, sl st in next ch] 11 times. Fasten off.

Arm
Make 2.

Row 1: With cream, ch 2, sc in 2nd ch from hook, turn. *(1 st)*

Row 2: Ch 1, 3 sc in st, turn. *(3 sts)*

Row 3: Ch 1, sc in each st across, change color to plum in last st, turn. Fasten off cream.

Rows 4–8: Ch 1, sc in each st across, turn.

Row 9: Ch 1, sk first st st, sc in each rem st across. Fasten off. *(2 sts)*

Edging

Hold Arm with foundation ch at top, join cream in end of row 3 at right edge, ch 1, sc evenly sp around outer edge of cream section, changing color to plum in last st, sc evenly sp around plum section, join in beg sc. Fasten off both colors.

Finishing

Sew Bottom to bottom of Princess. Referring to photo for shapes and color, cut out eyes and mouth from felt and glue to head of Princess.

Stuff Hair Bun lightly and sew to back of head.

Sew Crown around top of head and sew Collar around neck.

Sew Arm to each side of Princess.

Frog

Bottom Ring

Rnd 1: With medium thyme, ch 42, **join** *(see Pattern Notes)* to form ring, ch 1, sc in each ch around, join in beg sc, turn. *(42 sts)*

Rnds 2–78: Ch 1, sc in each st around, join in beg sc, turn. At end of last rnd, fasten off.

Stuff lightly and sew ends tog to form a ring.

Leg
Make 2.

Rnd 1: With medium thyme, ch 24, join to form a ring, turn, ch 1, sc in each ch around, join in beg sc, turn. *(24 sts)*

Rnds 2–20: Ch 1, sc in each st around, join in beg sc, turn.

Rnd 21: Ch 1, [sk next st, sc in each of next 5 sts] around, join in beg sc, turn. *(20 sts)*

Rnd 22: Ch 1, [sk next st, sc in each of next 4 sts] around, join in beg sc, turn. *(16 sts)*

Rnd 23: Ch 1, sc in each of next 6 sts, hdc in next st, 2 dc in next st, 3 tr in next st, 2 dc in next st, hdc in next st, sc in each of last 5 sts, join in beg sc, turn. *(20 sts)*

Rnd 24: Ch 1, sc in each of next 5 sts, [5 dc in next st, sl st in each of next 2 sts] 3 times, sc in each of last 6 sts, join in beg sc. Fasten off. *(32 sts)*

Foot Bottom
Make 2.

Rnd 1: With medium thyme, ch 6, sc in 2nd ch from hook, sc in each of next 3 chs, 3 sc in last ch, working in unused lps on opposite side of foundation ch, sc in each of next 3 chs, 2 sc in last ch, join in beg sc, turn. *(12 sts)*

Rnd 2: Ch 1, 2 sc in each of next 2 sts, sc in each of next 3 sts, 2 dc in next st, 3 tr in next st, 2 dc in next st, sc in each of next 3 sts, 2 sc in last st, join in beg sc, turn. *(19 sts)*

Rnd 3: Sl st in each of next 5 sts, [5 dc in next st, sl st each of next 2 sts] 3 times, sl st in each of last 5 sts. Fasten off.

Center Ring
Rnd 1: With frosty green, ch 22, join to form a ring, ch 1, sc in each ch around, join in beg sc, turn. *(22 sts)*

Rnds 2–68: Ch 1, sc in each st around, join in beg sc, turn. At end of last rnd, fasten off.

Stuff lightly and sew ends tog to form a ring.

Arm
Make 2.

Rnd 1: With frosty green, ch 24, join to form a ring, turn, ch 1, sc in each ch around, join in beg sc, turn. *(24 sts)*

Rnds 2–10: Ch 1, sc in each st around, join in beg sc, turn.

Rnd 11: Ch 1, [sk next st, sc in each of next 5 sts] around, join in beg sc, turn. *(20 sts)*

Rnds 12 & 13: Ch 1, sc in each st around, join in beg sc, turn.

Rnd 14: Ch 1, [sk next st, sc in each of next 4 sts] around, join in beg sc, turn. *(16 sts)*

Rnds 15 & 16: Ch 1, sc in each st around, join in beg sc, turn.

Rnd 17: Ch 1, sc in each of next 6 sts, hdc in next st, 2 dc in next st, 3 tr in next st, 2 dc in next st, hdc in next st, sc in each of last 5 sts, join in beg sc, turn. *(20 sts)*

Rnd 18: Ch 1, sc in each of next 5 sts, [5 dc in next st, sl st in each of next 2 sts] 3 times, sc in each of last 6 sts, join in beg sc. Fasten off. *(32 sts)*

Arm Bottom
Make 2.

With frosty green, work same as Foot Bottom.

Top Ring
Rnd 1: With medium thyme, ch 26, join to form a ring, turn, ch 1, sc in each ch around, join in beg sc, turn. *(26 sts)*

Rnds 2–62: Ch 1, sc in each st around, join in beg sc, turn. At end of last rnd, fasten off.

Stuff lightly and sew ends tog to form a ring.

Inner Eye
Make 2.

Rnd 1: With white, ch 2, 8 sc in 2nd ch from hook, join in beg sc, turn. *(8 sts)*

Rnd 2: Ch 1, 2 sc in each st around, join in beg sc, turn. *(16 sts)*

Rnds 3–5: Ch 1, sc in each st around, join in beg sc, turn. At end of last rnd, fasten off.

Back of Eye
Make 2.

Rnd 1: With medium thyme, ch 2, 10 sc in 2nd ch from hook, join in beg sc, turn. *(10 sts)*

Rnd 2: Ch 1, 2 sc in each st around, join in beg sc, turn. *(20 sts)*

Rnds 3–5: Ch 1, sc in each st around, join in beg sc, turn. At end of last rnd, fasten off.

Finishing
Sew 1 Foot Bottom to bottom of each Leg. Stuff lightly and sew to each side of Bottom Ring.

Sew 1 Arm Bottom to bottom of each Arm and sew 1 Arm to each side of Center Ring.

Sew 1 Inner Eye to each Back of Eye, stuffing lightly. Cut 2 1-inch circles from black felt and cut a pie-shaped wedge out of each. Glue felt eyes to white part of eyes. Sew finished Eyes to top edge of Top Ring.

With red and using **backstitch** *(see illustration)*, embroider mouth on Top Ring. ●

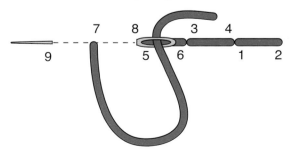

Backstitch

UFO Alien

Skill Level

◼◼◻◻ **EASY**

Finished Measurement

11 inches tall

Materials

- Red Heart Super Saver medium (worsted) weight acrylic yarn (7 oz/364 yds/198g per skein): **4 MEDIUM**
  - 1 skein each #322 pale yellow and #400 grey heather
  - 200 yds #312 black and #672 spring green
- Size H/8/5mm crochet hook or size needed to obtain gauge
- Tapestry needle
- Small amounts black and white felt
- Craft glue
- Polyester fiberfill

Gauge

4 sc = 1 inch; 3 sc rows = 1 inch

Pattern Notes

Weave in ends as work progresses.

Join with slip stitch as indicated unless otherwise stated.

After changing color, drop old color unless otherwise stated.

Chain-3 at beginning of round counts as a double crochet unless otherwise stated.

Alien

Rnd 1: Starting at top with green, ch 2, 8 sc in 2nd ch from hook, **join** *(see Pattern Notes)* in first st to form a ring, turn. *(8 sts)*

Rnd 2: Ch 1, sc in each st around, join in beg sc, turn.

Rnd 3: Ch 1, [sk next st, sc in next st] around, join in beg sc, turn. *(4 sts)*

Rnd 4: Ch 1, sc in each st around, join in beg sc, turn.

Rnd 5: Ch 1, [2 sc in next st, sc in next st] around, join in beg sc, turn. *(6 sts)*

Rnd 6: Ch 1, [2 sc in next st, sc in each of next 2 sts] around, join in beg sc, turn. *(8 sts)*

Rnd 7: Ch 1, [2 sc in next st, sc in each of next 3 sts] around, join in beg sc, turn. *(10 sts)*

Rnd 8: Ch 1, [2 sc in next st, sc in each of next 4 sts] around, join in beg sc, turn. *(12 sts)*

Rnd 9: Rep rnd 4.

Rnd 10: Ch 1, [2 sc in next st, sc in each of next 4 sts] around, join in beg sc, turn. *(18 sts)*

Rnd 11: Ch 1, [2 sc in next st, sc in each of next 2 sts] around, join in beg sc, turn. *(24 sts)*

Rnds 12 & 13: Rep rnd 4.

Rnd 14: Ch 1, [sk next st, sc in each of next 3 sts] around, join in beg sc, turn. *(18 sts)*

Rnd 15: Rep rnd 4.

Rnd 16: Ch 1, [sk next st, sc in each of next 2 sts] around, join in beg sc, turn. *(12 sts)*

Rnds 17–19: Rep rnd 4. At end of last rnd, **change color** *(see Stitch Guide and Pattern Notes)* to gray in last st, turn. Fasten off green.

Rnd 20: Ch 1, 2 sc in each st around, join in beg sc, turn. *(24 sts)*

Stuff with fiberfill.

Rnd 21: Ch 1, [2 sc in next st, sc in each of next 5 sts] around, join in beg sc, turn. *(28 sts)*

Rnds 22–26: Rep rnd 4.

Rnd 27: Ch 1, [2 sc in next st, sc in each of next 6 sts] around, join in beg sc, turn. *(32 sts)*

Rnds 28 & 29: Rep rnd 4.

Rnd 30: Ch 1, [2 sc in next st, sc in each of next 7 sts] around, join in beg sc, turn. *(36 sts)*

Rnds 31–34: Rep rnd 4.

Rnd 35: Ch 1, [2 sc in next st, sc in each of next 5 sts] around, join in beg sc, turn. *(42 sts)*

Rnds 36–43: Rep rnd 4. At end of last rnd, change color to yellow in last st. Fasten off gray.

Rnd 44: Ch 3 *(see Pattern Notes)*, dc in same st as beg ch-3, dc in next st, [2 dc in next st, dc in next st] around, join in 3rd ch of beg ch-3, turn. *(63 sts)*

Rnd 45: Ch 3, dc in same st as beg ch-3, dc in each of next 2 sts, [2 dc in next st, dc in each of next 2 sts] around, join in 3rd ch of beg ch-3. Fasten off. *(84 sts)*

Finish stuffing.

Bottom

Rnd 1: With yellow, ch 4, join to form a ring, 12 sc in ring, join in beg sc, turn. *(12 sts)*

Rnds 2 & 3: Ch 1, [2 sc in next st, sc in next st] around, join in beg sc, turn. *(27 sts at end of last rnd)*

Rnd 4: Ch 1, [2 sc in next st, sc in each of next 2 sts] around, join in beg sc, turn. *(36 sts)*

Rnd 5: Ch 1, [2 sc in next st, sc in each of next 2 sts] around, join in beg sc, turn. *(45 sts)*

Rnd 6: Ch 3, dc in each st around, join in 3rd ch of beg ch-3, turn.

Rnd 7: Ch 3, [2 dc in next st, dc in each of next 3 sts] around, join in 3rd ch of beg ch-3, turn. *(56 sts)*

Rnd 8: Ch 3, dc in same st as beg ch-3, dc in each of next 3 sts, [2 dc in next st, dc in each of next 3 sts] around, join in 3rd ch of beg ch-3. Fasten off. *(70 sts)*

Arm
Make 2.

Row 1: With green, ch 2, sc in 2nd ch from hook, turn. *(1 st)*

Row 2: Ch 1, 3 sc in st, turn. *(3 sts)*

Row 3: Ch 1, sc in each st across, changing color to gray in last st, turn. Fasten off green.

Rows 4–8: Ch 1, sc in each st across, turn.

Row 9: Ch 1, sk first st, sc in each rem st across. Fasten off. *(2 sts)*

Edging
Hold Arm with foundation ch at top, join green in end of row 3 at right edge, ch 1, sc evenly sp around outer edge of green section, changing color to gray in last st, sc evenly sp around gray section, join in beg sc. Fasten off both colors.

Collar

Row 1: With yellow, ch 2, sc in 2nd ch from hook, turn. *(1 st)*

Note: *Work rem rows in **back lps** (see Stitch Guide).*

Rows 2–7: Ch 1, sc in sc, turn.

Row 8: Ch 1, 2 sc in sc, turn. *(2 sts)*

Row 9: Ch 1, 2 sc in each sc, turn. *(4 sts)*

Row 10: Ch 1, 2 sc in first st, sc in each rem st across, turn. *(5 sts)*

Row 11: Ch 1, sc in each of first 4 sts, 2 sc in last st, turn. *(6 sts)*

Rows 12–24: Ch 1, sc in each st across, turn.

Row 25: Ch 1, sk first st, sc in each rem st across, turn. *(5 sts)*

Row 26: Ch 1, sc in each of first 3 sts, sk next st, sc in last st, turn. *(4 sts)*

Row 27: Ch 1, sk first st, sc in next st, sk next st, sc in next st, turn. *(2 sts)*

Row 28: Ch 1, sk first st, sc in last st, turn. *(1 st)*

Rows 29–35: Ch 1, sc in sc, turn. At end of last row, fasten off.

Finishing

Sew Bottom to bottom of Alien.

Sew 1 Arm to each side of Alien.

Sew Collar around Alien at neck, meeting at a point in center of chest. Cut 3 large white ovals and 3 small black ovals from felt. Glue black ovals to white ovals for eyes. Referring to photo for placement, glue eyes to face. Cut thin line of black felt and glue to face for mouth.

UFO

Bottom Ring

Rnd 1: With gray, ch 42, **join** *(see Pattern Notes)* to form ring, ch 1, sc in each ch around, join in beg sc, turn. *(42 sts)*

Rnds 2–78: Ch 1, sc in each st around, join in beg sc, turn. At end of last rnd, fasten off.

Stuff lightly and sew ends tog to form a ring.

Window
Make 9.

Rnd 1: With yellow, ch 2, 8 sc in 2nd ch from hook, join in beg sc, turn. *(8 sts)*

Rnd 2: Ch 1, 2 sc in each st around, join in beg sc. Fasten off. *(16 sts)*

Center Ring

Rnd 1: With yellow, ch 22, join to form a ring, ch 1, sc in each ch around, join in beg sc, turn. *(22 sts)*

Rnds 2–68: Ch 1, sc in each st around, join in beg sc, turn. At end of last rnd, fasten off.

Stuff lightly and sew ends tog to form a ring.

Long Window

Rnd 1: With gray, ch 20, sc in 2nd ch from hook, sc in each of next 17 chs, 3 sc in last ch, working in unused lps on opposite side of foundation ch, sc in each of next 17 chs, 2 sc in last ch, join in beg sc, turn. *(40 sts)*

Rnd 2: Ch 1, 2 sc in each of first 2 sts, sc in each of next 17 sts, 2 sc in each of next 3 sts, sc in each of next 17 sts, 2 sc last st, join in beg sc. Fasten off. *(46 sts)*

Top Ring

Rnd 1: With yellow, ch 26, join to form a ring, turn, ch 1, sc in each ch around, join in beg sc, turn. *(26 sts)*

Rnds 2–62: Ch 1, sc in each st around, join in beg sc, turn. At end of last rnd, fasten off.

Stuff lightly and sew ends tog to form a ring.

Medium Window
Make 3.

Rnd 1: With gray, ch 6, sc in 2nd ch from hook, sc in each of next 3 chs, 3 sc in last ch, working in unused lps on opposite side of foundation ch, sc in each of next 3 chs, 2 sc in last ch, turn. *(12 sts)*

Rnd 2: Ch 1, 2 sc in each of first 2 sts, sc in each of next 3 sts, 2 sc in each of next 3 sts, sc in each of next 3 sts, 2 sc last st, join in beg sc, turn. *(18 sts)*

Rnd 3: Ch 1, 2 sc in each of first 2 sts, sc in each of next 3 sts, 2 sc in each of next 6 sts, sc in each of next 3 sts, 2 sc in each of last 4 sts, join in beg sc. Fasten off. *(30 sts)*

Finishing
Sew Windows around Bottom Ring.

Sew Long Window to center of Center Ring.

Sew Medium Windows to Top Ring, alternating positions. ●

Baker Man
Continued from page 15

Cupcake

Bottom Ring
Rnd 1: With red, ch 42, join to form a ring, ch 1, sc in each ch around, join in beg sc, turn. *(42 sts)*

Rnds 2–78: Ch 1, sc in each st around, join in beg sc, turn. At end of last rnd, fasten off.

Stuff and sew ends tog to form a ring.

Center Cake Ring
Rnd 1: With café latte, ch 22, join to form a ring, ch 1, sc in each ch around, join in beg sc, turn. *(22 sts)*

Rnds 2–68: Ch 1, sc in each st around, join in beg sc, turn. At end of last rnd, fasten off.

Stuff and sew ends tog to form a ring.

White Icing Ring
Rnd 1: With white, ch 26, join to form a ring, turn, ch 1, sc in each ch around, join in beg sc, turn. *(26 sts)*

Rnds 2–62: Ch 1, sc in each st around, join in beg sc, turn. At end of last rnd, fasten off.

Stuff and sew ends tog to form a ring.

Finishing
Cut small bits of different-color felt and randomly glue to top of White Icing Ring to look like sprinkles. ●

STITCH GUIDE

STITCH ABBREVIATIONS

beg	begin/begins/beginning
bpdc	back post double crochet
bpsc	back post single crochet
bptr	back post treble crochet
CC	contrasting color
ch(s)	chain(s)
ch-	refers to chain or space previously made (i.e., ch-1 space)
ch sp(s)	chain space(s)
cl(s)	cluster(s)
cm	centimeter(s)
dc	double crochet (singular/plural)
dc dec	double crochet 2 or more stitches together, as indicated
dec	decrease/decreases/decreasing
dtr	double treble crochet
ext	extended
fpdc	front post double crochet
fpsc	front post single crochet
fptr	front post treble crochet
g	gram(s)
hdc	half double crochet
hdc dec	half double crochet 2 or more stitches together, as indicated
inc	increase/increases/increasing
lp(s)	loop(s)
MC	main color
mm	millimeter(s)
oz	ounce(s)
pc	popcorn(s)
rem	remain/remains/remaining
rep(s)	repeat(s)
rnd(s)	round(s)
RS	right side
sc	single crochet (singular/plural)
sc dec	single crochet 2 or more stitches together, as indicated
sk	skip/skipped/skipping
sl st(s)	slip stitch(es)
sp(s)	space(s)/spaced
st(s)	stitch(es)
tog	together
tr	treble crochet
trtr	triple treble
WS	wrong side
yd(s)	yard(s)
yo	yarn over

YARN CONVERSION

OUNCES TO GRAMS		GRAMS TO OUNCES	
1	28.4	25	⅞
2	56.7	40	1⅔
3	85.0	50	1¾
4	113.4	100	3½

UNITED STATES		UNITED KINGDOM
sl st (slip stitch)	=	sc (single crochet)
sc (single crochet)	=	dc (double crochet)
hdc (half double crochet)	=	htr (half treble crochet)
dc (double crochet)	=	tr (treble crochet)
tr (treble crochet)	=	dtr (double treble crochet)
dtr (double treble crochet)	=	ttr (triple treble crochet)
skip	=	miss

Single crochet decrease (sc dec): (Insert hook, yo, draw lp through) in each of the sts indicated, yo, draw through all lps on hook.

Example of 2-sc dec

Half double crochet decrease (hdc dec): (Yo, insert hook, yo, draw lp through) in each of the sts indicated, yo, draw through all lps on hook.

Example of 2-hdc dec

Reverse single crochet (reverse sc): Ch 1, sk first st, working from left to right, insert hook in next st from front to back, draw up lp on hook, yo and draw through both lps on hook.

Chain (ch): Yo, pull through lp on hook.

Single crochet (sc): Insert hook in st, yo, pull through st, yo, pull through both lps on hook.

Double crochet (dc): Yo, insert hook in st, yo, pull through st, [yo, pull through 2 lps] twice.

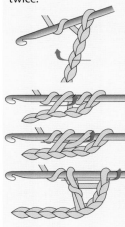

Double crochet decrease (dc dec): (Yo, insert hook, yo, draw lp through, yo, draw through 2 lps on hook) in each of the sts indicated, yo, draw through all lps on hook.

Example of 2-dc dec

Front loop (front lp) Back loop (back lp)

Front Loop Back Loop

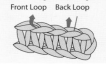

Front post stitch (fp): Back post stitch (bp): When working post st, insert hook from right to left around post of st on previous row.

Back Front

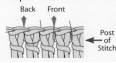

Post of Stitch

Half double crochet (hdc): Yo, insert hook in st, yo, pull through st, yo, pull through all 3 lps on hook.

Double treble crochet (dtr): Yo 3 times, insert hook in st, yo, pull through st, [yo, pull through 2 lps] 4 times.

Treble crochet decrease (tr dec): Holding back last lp of each st, tr in each of the sts indicated, yo, pull through all lps on hook.

Example of 2-tr dec

Slip stitch (sl st): Insert hook in st, pull through both lps on hook.

Chain color change (ch color change) Yo with new color, draw through last lp on hook.

Double crochet color change (dc color change) Drop first color, yo with new color, draw through last 2 lps of st.

Treble crochet (tr): Yo twice, insert hook in st, yo, pull through st, [yo, pull through 2 lps] 3 times.

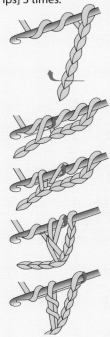

Metric Conversion Charts

METRIC CONVERSIONS

yards	x	.9144	=	metres (m)
yards	x	91.44	=	centimetres (cm)
inches	x	2.54	=	centimetres (cm)
inches	x	25.40	=	millimetres (mm)
inches	x	.0254	=	metres (m)

centimetres	x	.3937	=	inches
metres	x	1.0936	=	yards

INCHES INTO MILLIMETRES & CENTIMETRES (Rounded off slightly)

inches	mm	cm	inches	cm	inches	cm	inches	cm
1/8	3	0.3	5	12.5	21	53.5	38	96.5
1/4	6	0.6	5 1/2	14	22	56	39	99
3/8	10	1	6	15	23	58.5	40	101.5
1/2	13	1.3	7	18	24	61	41	104
5/8	15	1.5	8	20.5	25	63.5	42	106.5
3/4	20	2	9	23	26	66	43	109
7/8	22	2.2	10	25.5	27	68.5	44	112
1	25	2.5	11	28	28	71	45	114.5
1 1/4	32	3.2	12	30.5	29	73.5	46	117
1 1/2	38	3.8	13	33	30	76	47	119.5
1 3/4	45	4.5	14	35.5	31	79	48	122
2	50	5	15	38	32	81.5	49	124.5
2 1/2	65	6.5	16	40.5	33	84	50	127
3	75	7.5	17	43	34	86.5		
3 1/2	90	9	18	46	35	89		
4	100	10	19	48.5	36	91.5		
4 1/2	115	11.5	20	51	37	94		

KNITTING NEEDLES CONVERSION CHART

Canada/U.S.	0	1	2	3	4	5	6	7	8	9	10	10½	11	13	15
Metric (mm)	2	2¼	2¾	3¼	3½	3¾	4	4½	5	5½	6	6½	8	9	10

CROCHET HOOKS CONVERSION CHART

Canada/U.S.	1/B	2/C	3/D	4/E	5/F	6/G	8/H	9/I	10/J	10½/K	N
Metric (mm)	2.25	2.75	3.25	3.5	3.75	4.25	5	5.5	6	6.5	9.0

Annie's® *Playtime Stackers* is published by Annie's, 306 East Parr Road, Berne, IN 46711. Printed in USA. Copyright © 2014, 2015 Annie's. All rights reserved. This publication may not be reproduced in part or in whole without written permission from the publisher.

RETAIL STORES: If you would like to carry this publication or any other Annie's publication, visit AnniesWSL.com.

Every effort has been made to ensure that the instructions in this publication are complete and accurate. We cannot, however, take responsibility for human error, typographical mistakes or variations in individual work. Please visit AnniesCustomerService.com to check for pattern updates.

ISBN: 978-1-57367-599-4

3 4 5 6 7 8 9 10 11 12